Teenagers Talk About Grief

Teenagers
Talk
About
Grief

June Cerza Kolf

BAKER BOOK HOUSE
Grand Rapids, Michigan 49516

For
Sharon Frances Patton,

whose bright smile I shall
always miss

and
her daughter,

Anne Tillotson

Heartfelt thanks to the special people who shared their stories with me and who supported, encouraged, and assisted me with their time, thoughts, prayers, listening ears, editing, or prodding.

God bless you.

Ruth Hunter
Cindy Iacobellis
Mary Justice
Brandi Pursley
Ann Smart
Kathy Kolf Spillar
Bob and Gloria Willis
JoAnne Word

Contents

Prologue

I answered the telephone and heard my mother, who was calling long distance from Illinois.

"Hi, June. I have some sad news. Sharon died yesterday."

While I sat completely stunned, letting this information soak into my brain, she went on with her news. I interrupted her mid-sentence.

"What do you mean, Sharon died," I said rather sharply. "I saw her a few months ago, and she was fine. In fact I spoke to her a few weeks ago, and she was fine then, too. She can't have died."

"Well, she had a blood clot, I think it was, and she went very fast."

Mom continued to talk, but I was only half listening. My mind was racing with scenes from my last visit with Sharon, our last conversation, my last letter to her. It was unthinkable that she was no longer alive. I had known her since we were in the sixth grade together. Grandmothers and grandfathers died, not childhood friends. Maybe other people's friends died, but not mine.

Then my racing mind came to a sharp halt as I remembered Sharon's daughter. I could feel my heart splinter into tiny fragments as I thought about Anne, the one consistently bright spot in Sharon's life. Sharon's face always lit up when she mentioned Anne. She couldn't believe this terrific kid was her daughter. "I don't know what I did to deserve her," she would say over and over again, shaking her head in wonder.

Sharon had been faced with more than her share of problems in life, but she never let them get her down. She offered a listening ear to friends or strangers, and she gave away material possessions with never a second thought. Her face was generally adorned with a broad smile, and she was a pleasure to be near. With her happy-go-lucky personality she acted as if nothing much mattered except for Anne, her greatest joy.

I have three daughters of my own, so I nodded in agreement when Sharon got all silly about Anne. However, having three daughters and a husband divided my love by four. Sharon's love was all lumped together for her only child. Wow! It was hard for me to comprehend. But now Anne no longer had her mother.

I happen to be a writer with two published books about grief, so my initial thought was to head to the bookstore in search of a book for Anne to help her deal with her mother's sudden death. No luck. There was not a single book on the shelves that was written especially for teenagers who are grieving.

I checked the computers at the stores and searched in the libraries. I asked around town. Nothing. I wrung my hands. Meanwhile, I wrote a letter to Anne. While I was writing, it occurred to me that maybe the Lord was whispering a message to me. I stopped and listened carefully, and I believe he told me to write a book for grieving teenagers.

I had no personal experience with death as a teenager, so I interviewed people who had experienced the death of a loved one while in their teen years. When I began looking for people to interview, I was amazed at how eager everyone was to help me. As I approached these people, I felt guilty about making them reopen their wounds. I apologized, and the response was always the same, "You don't need to feel guilty or sorry, June. It feels good to talk about it." One woman told me she had been waiting fourteen years to find a person who would listen to her story. Listen I did.

In my interviews with teens, the same "adult" feelings about death surfaced again and again—shock, anger, guilt, loneliness, depression, bargaining, and physical symptoms. The difference was in the response. Teens need to feel like their peers. Anonymity is vitally important, so they hide their true feelings. I also discovered that help is not as readily available for teenagers as it is for adults. Support groups are few and far between. For financial reasons, teens cannot simply decide they need counseling and pick up the telephone and make an appointment. School counselors, when available, do assist, but, teens' lives and resources are controlled to a great degree by their parents or guardians. Young people are not equipped to search out professional help or initiate support systems.

At the same time teens feel compelled to act brave to turn attention away from themselves. They keep their feelings carefully hidden so that even when help is available, no one is aware that they need it. For as much as death is coming out of the closet these days, it is not doing so for young people. Death continues to be a taboo subject, and where help should be available, a large void remains instead.

Not only is there a need for books and reading material, there is also a great urgency for public awareness and understanding. We all must turn listening ears toward the young people at funerals and in the weeks following their loss. Teenagers experience emotions in the extreme, often with no past experiences to draw on as a frame of reference. A listening friend, a support group, adequate resource materials, or private counseling can soothe a breaking heart and help it to mend more quickly.

This book is the result of my own broken heart. It is the bandage that I used to soothe my hurt. As I began to accept the death of my friend, I needed to turn that loss into something meaningful. Sharon had been embarrassingly proud of my writing successes and supportive of even my simplest efforts. She acted as if I could do anything I attempted, and it gave me the incentive to keep plugging away. I can picture her looking over my shoulder right now with her big, broad smile and saying, "Go for it, June."

Okay, Lord, I get the message. I'll write this one for Sharon!

1

Acknowledgment

"When I look into the mirror I'm surprised to see that I still look the same. I have all these new thoughts and feelings that make me feel like a stranger. One minute I feel fine, and the next I'm on the verge of tears. I get angry for no reason and can barely control myself. I don't understand what's going on," Gregg told me with a puzzled look on his face. "My dad was sick a long time, and I knew I would feel real sad when he died, but I wasn't prepared for all this other stuff."

The death of a loved one can throw a person not only into a world of sadness, but also one of unfamiliarity that is filled with indecision, anger, guilt, depression, and tears. Young people experience grief intensely whether the loss is a brother or sister, a best friend, a parent, or a grandparent. Each loss is different and every person is unique, but there are certain feelings that almost everyone experiences.

When a loved one dies, you are forced to think about

your own fragile life and the lives of the people close to you. Death becomes a reality, not merely something that happens to other people. Death brings on sadness; life seems unfair. You feel as if you have been treated unjustly by God. You envy others who have not had to suffer a loss, and then you feel guilty over the envy. You are assaulted with so many new emotions that you simply cannot sort them all out. You feel misplaced and no longer safe. Fear overcomes you for no known reason. You ask yourself how a day can make such a difference. Actually, how can the fraction of a minute make such an impact on your life? In an instant you are confronted with situations that you never expected to face. Life is no longer the same and never will be again. Even though the nightly news reports click off death tolls hourly, and newspapers have story after story relating to death, up until now it was something that happened to other people, not you.

You feel a red-hot rage seething inside and have no idea of how to release it. You have no energy, no desire to do anything. You want to turn the clock back and restore your world to the way it was before this awful change took place in your life. But you are powerless. You cannot control this dreadful situation you have been thrust into through no choice of your own.

You go around in circles, your moods swing crazily back and forth, up and down. *Am I losing it,* you wonder.

No, you are not "losing it." You are simply experiencing grief—an unplanned for, unwished for, undesirable condition. It is a condition that is the result of loving someone. Anyone who loves another person is taking a chance on someday being faced with grief. The only way to avoid it is to never love anyone. You may even wonder if the love was worth it. You wonder if these thoughts and feelings are normal.

What Is "Normal"?

These strange new feelings you are experiencing are perfectly normal. You are not "going crazy." The important difference between normal and abnormal feelings and behavior is in the extent and length of time they continue. For example, it is perfectly normal to wish you were dead when you are suffering from a loss, as long as those thoughts are fleeting and not constant. If you are actually looking for methods to end your life, then it is a situation that needs to be dealt with by a professional. It is no longer normal behavior.

If you have no energy to move out of bed and no desire to see people on occasion, that is perfectly normal. If these moods go on for days at a time and affect your performance and grades, however, they are no longer a normal grief reaction.

If you sob long and hard, it is normal and healthy. Crying is nature's method of releasing pain when it can no longer be endured. Your tears are serving a purpose. They are soothing a troubled spirit. If the crying spells continue for months and are affecting your relationships and interfering with your daily life, then they are no longer normal.

It is natural for grieving people to feel cheated, that life is not fair, that they got a dirty deal. Angry feelings will crop up unexpectedly and need to be dealt with in an acceptable manner. If anger is out of control, repeatedly, it is no longer considered a response to grief but a problem that needs to be solved. One or two outbursts can be considered acceptable behavior because of the circumstances.

Feeling invisible is common. Fifteen-year-old Joe said, "The day of my grandma's funeral nobody looked at me or talked to me. I felt like I was invisible. When we went back to the house after the funeral, I decided to play a game with myself and pretend I actually was invisible. Sure enough, it worked. It made me feel a little better and made the time go by faster. At eight o'clock that night my dad looked up at me and said, 'Hey, Joe, don't you think it's time for bed?' *Eight* o'clock! Maybe invisible was better."

In the early days of grief, each family member is preoccupied, dealing with his or her own individual problems. The burden of grief is so heavy that it leaves no energy for helping others. Joe's dad was using all of his energy for his own survival, therefore he was unable to aid Joe or consider the way he might be feeling.

Other normal grief responses might be uncomfortable physical symptoms, guilt, bargaining, fear, loneliness, depression, shock, or denial. Shock is usually the first reaction that follows the news that a loved one has died.

Shock

Jamie was a freshman in high school and had been home sick for two days. The morning she returned to school she dashed out to her friend's car. Lynn, a neighbor a few years older, drove Scott and Jamie to school each day.

Scott and Jamie had started kindergarten together ten years before. Jamie had always felt safe walking to school with Scott. He protected her from strange dogs and the older kids. One windy day he saved her from a blowing tumbleweed. That particular day he stood in front of her so the prickly bush would not hit her little bare legs. As they got older, they rode their bikes to school together, racing down the street. This was the first year they were being driven to school. Arriving together made them feel less intimidated by the large, unfamiliar school. They still walked home together each afternoon because Lynn stayed for band practice.

As Jamie climbed into the car she casually asked, "Where's Scott, today?"

Her friend leaned over and whispered, "You mean you

haven't heard? Scott is dead. He was killed by a drunk driver when he was walking home from school yesterday." Often shocking news takes a while to get to people, and when they receive it they are totally unprepared.

"Oh, come on. That's not funny. Where is he really?" Then Jamie looked at Lynn and realized it was not a joke. Lynn's eyes were filled with tears. Still Jamie couldn't believe it. There had to be some mistake. Maybe this was just a bad dream.

At school many of the kids who had just received the news were crying. It was the first time many of them were touched by the death of someone close. Students were hugging and roaming the halls aimlessly. Jamie went to her classes. She has very little recollection, however, of anything that took place after the hugging and crying.

"I remember feeling like I was floating around in a thick fog. The whole day seemed unreal. My eyes kept filling with tears that I seemed unable to control. I felt sick to my stomach and was unable to eat."

Jamie was in shock. The very first stage of grief is shock or denial. When a person is unexpectedly faced with a wound that is too painful to absorb all at once, the body releases a natural anesthetic for protection. The natural anesthetic arrives in the form of shock. The shock wears off little by little, allowing the body to absorb the news in small doses that it can handle. Shock is what gets people through agonizing situations and experiences.

While in shock, people often function in a manner that looks normal to others. But they will feel like they are moving about in a dream or a haze. Life has an unreal quality to it. After some time has elapsed, the body is better equipped to face the pain, so the shock gradually wears off, making the pain more apparent. Like a wound it is too soon to touch it, but one can look at the pain and acknowledge that it exists.

Once the loss is acknowledged and the numbness begins to wear off, other unfamiliar responses, such as guilt, will appear.

Guilt

Jamie began to feel guilty after the shock wore off a little bit.

"If I had gone to school that day, Scott would not have been walking home alone. I would have seen the car and warned him." Jamie heaped the guilt on herself, unreasonably thinking the entire accident had been her fault. Guilt, resulting from feeling responsible for the death, is very common in the early stages of grief. At this point Jamie needed to talk to someone she trusted. Expressing these thoughts verbally often clears the air as people hear how irrational they are being.

As the days went by, Jamie remembered every cross word she had ever spoken to Scott. I should have been nicer, she kept thinking.

In her intense grief, Jamie forgot that everyone says things they don't mean. Best friends say mean things. Brothers and sisters fight. Children get angry with their parents. We shout, "I hate you" and "I wish you were dead," with never a second thought. That is, until the friend, sibling, or parent should happen to die. Then every mean and nasty word or thought washes over us, trying to drown us. We wish we could take back the hateful words, but it's too late to do that. The words cannot be taken back. The past cannot be changed. All we can do is learn from the experience and start over fresh from that point on.

Eventually Jamie stopped blaming herself and was able to dig out the happy memories of Scott. She made a collage of pictures taken over the years and hung it on her bedroom wall. She spent many hours comforting Scott's family. She was able to fill the empty spot in their lives a tiny bit, and it helped ease her own loneliness, too.

Denial

In addition to shock, denial often takes up residence with grieving people.

Tami said, "I find myself doing strange things since my mother died. I play a lot of pretend games when I'm at school, I pretend as though nothing has changed. I think about my mom and what she will do and say when I get home from school and I actually have conversations with her even though she has been gone for four months."

Denial, like shock, is another form of self-protection. When the pain of your loss becomes too much to bear, you try to deny that it exists. This may work for the time being but eventually the truth comes crashing down. For instance, when Tami walked in the door after school, she was forced to admit all over again that her mother had died. Every day she tried to prepare herself as she entered the house, but it took months before she was able to face it without tears.

Denial will sneak up as the shock wears off, and the two feelings often trade back and forth while your mind and body are gradually becoming accustomed to the changes in your life. Denial is normal as long as it does not continually take the place of reality.

Bargaining

You feel very fragile after experiencing the death of someone you love. You will feel mortal, possibly for the first time. "I never realized it was so easy to die. One minute you're alive and the next you're not. That could happen to me!" It is a foregone conclusion that one out of one people die. In other words, no one gets out of this life alive.

It's hard to admit that we are terminal. We breeze along thinking like Woody Allen, who once said, "I'm not afraid of death. I just don't want to be there when it happens to me." We all feel this way. Why think about it now? We can face it later on.

When someone close to us dies, we are forced to think about death. All of a sudden it is not some stranger's name in the obituary column; it is our own loved one's. The realization that someday it will be our name hits us over the head like a bucket of cement.

Every ache and pain becomes a concern. You worry about riding in a car. Accidents and illnesses become real in a way they never were before. Could my headache be a brain tumor? You begin to worry about your family and friends illogically. Should my grandpa be lifting those cartons or will it bring on a heart attack? Is my mother's cough the beginning of lung cancer? If she dies I'll be an orphan. What would happen to me? For the first time in your life you are afraid to board an airplane. After all, airplanes have been known to crash. If someone is five minutes late, you fear an accident.

With the awareness of mortality and as all these new fears attack you, bargaining may appear on the scene. You may bargain with yourself and you might even try to bargain with God: *If I'm real good, God, will you let me live long enough to go to college? If I stop arguing with my parents, will you keep them alive until I'm grown? If I jog every day maybe I won't have a heart attack like my dad did. If I get an "A" in English, maybe my grandpa won't die.*

These bargains may bring temporary comfort, but they hold no merit. Life and death cannot be outsmarted. All you can do is live each day to its fullest and try to make the best of whatever time you are given.

Bargaining is considered a normal stage of grief as long as it is kept in its proper perspective and does not take over your life. Bargains are wishful thinking and not something that people can control.

Anxiety

As you mourn the loss of a loved one, you are filled with fear and anxiety. You are afraid of everything and have a heavy, uneasy feeling. When asked what you are afraid of, you cannot explain it. You may notice shortness of breath, dizziness, a racing heart, a tingling sensation all over, difficulty swallowing, and an unexplained panic. Could you be afraid of your own death? Could you be afraid of facing life without your special person? You feel that if you could just put a name to the fear it would disappear. Instead it hovers just under the surface, never far away.

You dash about wildly, hoping to outsmart the invasion of fear, but it catches up to you no matter where you try to hide. It sneaks up and attacks when you are least expecting it, taking your breath away. It almost smothers you at night when you try to sleep. Sometimes it is large and looming, like an elephant trampling through your life. And sometimes it is like a rat gnawing away inside you. But whichever it is, anxiety is a companion nobody needs.

The best way to make it disappear is to talk or write about it. Or maybe it would be easier for you to talk into a cassette recorder. Fear is very shy, and when exposed to another person, it quietly disappears. Writing about anxiety can have the same effect. Fearful feelings expressed on paper can sometimes make them seem less threatening. Nobody needs to see what you have written or listen to what you have said. Relief results from the task of writing or talking.

Physical Symptoms

In addition to fear and anxiety, grieving people experience a vast array of physical discomforts. They may have indigestion, heartburn, diarrhea, loss of appetite, unquenchable thirst, headaches, breathing difficulties, a lump in the throat, difficulty swallowing, or chest pains. Stress can cause any number of these symptoms. Symptoms that are a great discomfort or are interfering with your daily work should be looked into by a physician. Usually the discomfort disappears by itself within a couple of weeks.

Sleeping disorders and nightmares may continue for a longer time. These can be controlled to some degree by getting into the proper frame of mind before bedtime. Practicing the relaxation techniques in the next chapter can also be very helpful. It is a good idea not to become overly stimulated just before bedtime, or to eat or drink items with an excess of sugar or caffeine. Proper diet and exercise can contribute to better sleeping. Often talking about a nightmare will work it out of the subconscious and stop it from recurring.

Loneliness

A natural symptom of grief is loneliness. When a person is no longer a part of your life, you will suffer great loneliness for them. You miss the spot they shared in your life, and you notice a big, black vacuum that nobody else can fill. Grief is actually the memory of a loved one who is no longer present.

Heather said she was filled with despair after her mother died. The loneliness wrapped itself around her like a blanket, isolating her from others. She felt as if her own importance had disappeared and nobody—anywhere—cared about her. She ached for her mother's smile of approval or one of her hugs. One day, when she was missing her mother terribly and was praying for answers, she realized that she had not really "lost" her mother.

"Her physical presence was gone from my life, but I had not *lost* her. I decided never to use that word again. I still had her love and all the happy memories of times we had shared. I had inherited her blue eyes and her sense of humor. Nobody could ever take those away from me. I also had photographs, letters she had written me, and her set of good china. From that day on, I felt better. I realized I was a very lucky person who had been blessed with an exceptional mom for fifteen years." Heather wisely compensated for her loneliness as best she could.

A young man told me that he often thought of his grandfather as being in the next room. "Someday I'll join him in that special room, but for now he's safe and sound while he waits close-by for me. We're still under the same roof; just not in the same room where we can see each other. I know he still loves me and wants good things to happen in my life."

It is always too soon for a loved one to die. My dad died six months before my first book was published. When my complimentary copies arrived and I held the first copy in my hands, I wasn't excited or pleased. Instead I burst into tears because my dad, also an author, had never gotten to hold my finished book in his hands. I was filled with sadness over the proud moment he was denied.

If he had lived to see my book, he still might have died before my two daughters got married. Or before he held his first great-grandchild. There is never a time when we are ready to let go of our loved one's presence. Is there any way to fill this empty spot that is left when someone we love dies?

You can fill the void with other people who need your love. You can search out new friends, isolated people in nursing homes, or support groups with other kids who have experienced the death of a loved one. Together you can ease each other's loneliness a little bit. You can also treasure happy memories and photographs and allow them to bring you comfort. These tactics will ease the pain a little bit, though they can never replace the person who is physically gone from your life.

2

Adjustment

Once the initial feelings have been experienced and the mind acknowledges that a loss has occurred, the period of adjustment begins. This time period is a little more difficult because now you are working without the natural anesthetic of shock to ease the pain. This is the time when you realize with a jolt that your loved one is not coming back. He will never sit in that chair across the table from you again or sleep in the bed down the hall.

You will have agonizing experiences when you reach for the phone to call your best friend to tell her your good news and be almost knocked breathless with the realization that she is no longer there to receive your calls. You wonder, *Will I ever get over this?*

Grief is not something you will "get over." It must be walked through—straight down the middle and out the other side. When you arrive there, you will be a stronger, different individual, better equipped to face any upheaval life can dish out.

Ignoring grief will not make it go away. It will remain intact until you decide to look at it, sort it out, work through it, and then put it to rest. If it is ignored, it will just continue to manifest itself in physical illnesses, eating disorders, temper tantrums, lack of concentration, or other disruptive ways.

How can you work out grief? Research shows that the best way to get rid of grief is to talk about it. As you talk about it, grief naturally works itself out. If you cannot find an understanding friend, sibling, parent, or counselor to talk with, then write down your feelings. They need to be aired out before they can be relinquished.

During the "working through period," you will look at others having a good time and resent it. You will ask, "Why did this have to happen to me?" This is the most common time for angry feelings to surface.

Anger

Steve tells about the experience he had following his father's death. After baseball practice one evening, he went to his car and discovered his keys locked inside. He was overcome with rage. He took the baseball bat he still had in his hand and smashed the car window. Then he threw the bat down and burst into tears. He got into his car, sat on all the broken glass, and sobbed.

"When I finished crying, I peeked around to see if anyone had seen me. Thank goodness I was the last one to leave the field. I had been feeling angry, but I thought I had it under control. I don't know where the explosion came from. It hit me like nothing I've ever felt before."

Steve's reaction was caused by unbearable stress and suppressed anger. Often when a father dies leaving behind a son, everyone tells the son that he must take over for the father: "Now, you're the man in the family. You'll have to take care of your mother and sisters."

This is too big a role for any young person to fill, and it is an unfair one. Nobody can fill another person's shoes or take his place. Steve had been hearing this statement and resenting it. He hated not having a dad and he agonized over the way his mother was suffering. He was tired of the tears, the indecision, the financial worries his mother put on his shoulders, and he was just plain tired of living. His internal computer was overloaded from the death of his father, and the silly incident with the car keys was all it took for him to explode.

Steve's mother was surprised when she heard about Steve's fit of anger. Before his father's death three months earlier, Steve had been even-tempered and docile. As a result of Steve's outburst, his mother became aware of his unresolved anger. She and Steve talked about the unrealistic demands being placed on him and his resulting anger. They began to work out some compromises and discussed ways to get rid of his anger.

Anger is the most common reaction to grief. It will crop up for a long time afterward. Anger may be felt toward the person who died and left you in this mess, or toward God for allowing it to happen. You may be angry at your friends who did not suffer the loss you did. You feel angry over every single big and little event in your life. You might even be angry at yourself for being angry.

Psychologists disagree about many theories, but on one point they agree unanimously: There is no such thing as a person who never gets angry—there are only those who suppress their anger. When anger is suppressed, it fizzes away inside, much like a can of soda pop that has been shaken up. The suppressed anger can produce migraines, ulcers, and/or a variety of psychosomatic problems if the pressure is not released. An angry person will explode unexpectedly, exactly as the soda can will, unless the anger is released in acceptable ways and channeled constructively.

If you are in touch with your feelings, you will be aware of times when you become angry or tense, and you can exert the effort to gradually expel your anger before it erupts. A brisk walk, a fast game of tennis, or a bike ride where you work up a sweat can relieve anger.

It is important to find a way to release anger in a manner that does not harm you or anyone else. Expressing your anger in words to an understanding person or writing your feelings down on paper can also release it in a constructive way.

Life Is Unfair

It is common to feel that life is not fair when you experience the death of a loved one. Several teenagers claimed that when one parent died they felt they had also lost their other parent.

"Mom was so busy thinking about Dad's death that she forgot all about me," Steve said. This is not unusual. Steve may have to find a parental substitute until his mother gets her bearings back. Steve's mother is dealing with her own painful moments. Steve needs to hang in there and realize his mother's lack of attention has nothing to do with her love for him. It is a bad time for the entire family, and his mother is coping as best she can right now.

When a brother or sister dies, the remaining children feel the parents would rather it had been them who died. The child who is gone becomes the prime focus in the household, making everyone else feel second best. The loss of a child goes against nature and takes a tremendous toll on parents' lives. Bereaved parents say it can take up to seven years before they feel human again.

"During the funeral everyone consoled my mom and dad. Nobody even talked to me. How come nobody remembers I lost my only sister?"

Sad, but a frequent occurrence. Adults often forget the young people at funerals. Little children are thought to be too young to understand, so they are shuffled aside or sent to stay elsewhere until the funeral is over. Nobody explains what is going on or offers them any consolation. Teenagers, too, are frequently ignored. In my book *How Can I Help?* I refer to these people as the "forgotten grievers." Unfortunately, there is no simple solution.

It is unwise to feel responsible for restoring your family's happiness following the death of a family member. It would be impossible to do. Only with each individual's personal grief work can happiness be restored. You may be required to take a backseat for a while—not because of anything you have done, but rather as a result of the grief work that is taking all the grievers' energy at this time. Before special occasions, a gentle reminder to ease any lapses in memory may be necessary.

"Hey, Mom, remember Friday is cheerleading tryouts. Want to come and watch them?" Or put an announcement on the refrigerator: *only twelve more shopping days 'til my birthday*. Attention span and memory retention are poor when people are grieving. Try not to take these lapses as a lack of love. The blame belongs to the grief, not the person grieving.

It is perfectly natural to wonder what the loss means in terms of your own life, but you may feel selfish even mentioning it. Will I still be able to go to college now that Dad is gone? Can we still afford a private school? Will I be able to get my license next year? Will we have to move? Will I have to change schools? These worries are natural, not selfish.

After the funeral is over, it is all right to mention that you wish to be included in making plans for the future. Let it be known that you have concerns and need to talk about them. It is also okay to remind a parent that you are mourning too, as long as it is done gently.

Depression

Depression is the natural reaction to a major loss. It is a sneaky emotion and comes carefully disguised so that it is not easy to recognize. Depression is the feeling that there is no reason to get out of bed in the morning. There is no joy in doing anything and no energy to expend. You feel empty and hollow.

"When my mother died, I felt I had nothing to live for," Karen said. "I felt I never wanted to get married because there was no one to help me choose a wedding dress. Dating seemed like a waste of time. Getting good grades didn't seem worth the effort anymore. Who would come to my graduation? I felt like my life had ended, too. It didn't make any difference that I had a dad, brothers, and sisters, and plenty of relatives and friends. For me, I was left all alone with no mother. It took a long time for me to realize that I had others who loved me."

Depression clouds your thinking. When you are depressed, your energy level is at zero. This lack of energy contributes to the inability to think clearly. It is simply too exhausting to work out solutions to a problem. It is easier to wallow around in misery. My friend, psychologist Dan Matzke, says, "Analysis leads to paralysis. It is easy to become so involved in analyzing a situation that we have no time to live each day. The healthy ratio of living to analyzing should be one to eight. For every eight hours we spend experiencing life we should spend only one hour analyzing. Otherwise life passes us by. Live one day at a time," he further suggests. Overanalyzing can add to depression.

There are several methods that may help ease you out of your depression.

Exercise

Although it is difficult to exercise when you are depressed, a good way to restore energy and begin to work through depression is with physical exercise. The recommended amount is twenty minutes a day, three times a week. I use a Christian aerobics tape. The music is so uplifting that it almost forces me to participate. By listening to the lyrics in the background, I can nourish my spirit at the same time I am exercising my body.

The first decision to participate in physical exercise is the most difficult; each time and each day gets easier. Set simple limits in the beginning, such as "I'll just walk to the corner today and give the dog a little exercise." Or ride your bike around the block one time with your little brother. A short bicycle ride or swimming laps with a friend will give your energy level a boost. Including another person or a pet makes the commitment seem easier.

Kathy Stevenson, in her article "Shoppercise," (*Redbook*, Nov. 1989) facetiously writes about basing her exercise program on her most enjoyable activity—shopping. "Would you rather do Jane Fonda's workout or spend two hours at Bullock's Department Store?" she asks. It lists calories burned and exercise received from browsing (150 calories/hour) up to hitting an after-Christmas sale (1,750 calories/hour). You can exercise your arm by pushing clothes rapidly along a clothes rack or doing calf raises while reaching over a counter to pay for your merchandise.

The article mentions that malls make it possible to exercise indoors when the weather is bad. Do your walking inside a mall, where you can peek at the window displays as you go along. When you walk the entire length, you can reward yourself with going into the stores for a closer look.

Although this article was being humorous, the idea does make sense. Combining an activity you enjoy with exercise is a good way to stick to your goals. It is healthy to take your mind off yourself and your problems for a little while as you perform a chosen task.

Nutrition

Good nutrition also aids in warding off depression. A car cannot go very far on an empty gas tank. Neither can you go far on a starved system. Good food strengthens the body and makes it better able to withstand the feelings of mourning without giving in quite as easily to depression.

People who are grieving have a tendency toward dehydration. They need to drink one-third more water than the average person, about eleven glasses a day. As emotions are speeded up, the body can become dehydrated. Extra water is needed as a preventative measure.

"I know I'm supposed to eat better, but I have no appetite," says ninety-pound Jenny. On the other hand her friend (who is overweight) cannot stop eating. Unfortunately, this is common. Small, frequent meals can sometimes solve both problems, but food choice is more important than quantity. Food should be nutritious. Some good snacks are raisins, fresh fruit or vegetables, popcorn, graham crackers, dried fruit, and granola.

Stay away from sugar, drugs, and alcohol. They make the depression more difficult to handle. Alcohol is a depressant, not a stimulant. It rushes to the brain, causing the central nervous system to become depressed. Feelings of sadness are escalated, increasing the depression rather than relieving it.

Rest

"When I try to fall asleep I have all sorts of trouble. And when I finally do sleep I have awful nightmares," Robb said. "I'd rather stay awake than have to experience those." When your system is depressed, sleep can be a problem. Allowing yourself to wind down an hour or so before bedtime can bring about a more relaxed state so your body can fall asleep. Heavy food, excessive exercise, stimulating conversation, loud music, and caffeine can detract from peaceful sleep.

If your mind begins to work overtime as soon as you settle down to sleep, you need to consciously turn it off. Picture a television set and turn the dial to change the channel to a soothing station or shut the set off completely. If thoughts are running wild in your mind, talk to them. Say, "Stop! I don't want to think about you anymore." This is called "thought interruption" and can be used whenever unpleasant thoughts take over your mind.

"I'm afraid to go to sleep. Maybe I won't wake up," Tom said after the death of his grandfather. Death and sleep often get confused. As young children we frequently hear the terms used interchangeably. "The dog is old and sick, so we are having him put to sleep." "Grandma is no longer with us. She has gone to sleep forever." We are told people who are dead will look just like they do when they are sleeping. The two words become tangled in our minds, often making us fear sleep when death has recently touched our lives. The way to counteract this reaction is to confront it. Realize that death and sleep are not the same. Use thought interruption or change the channels when necessary.

Sleeping pills may help a person fall asleep sooner, but they can interfere with normal sleep patterns and bring about severe problems. It is better to use natural means to obtain sleep. Warm milk, soft music, or a book of poetry can provide a relaxing situation. Reading the Bible, praying, or reciting Scripture verses are both relaxing and comforting. My preferred method for bringing about sleep is to sing hymns in my mind.

Nightmares are common. They will, in time, disappear. Talking about them with a trusted friend can help dispel their frightening quality. When sleep seems impossible, merely resting quietly has beneficial effects.

Tears

Crying is one of the healthiest reactions to grief. Tears are nature's way of washing away the pain. Studies have shown that tears shed in sadness have a different chemical makeup than tears of joy. It is possible that this substance actually has a calming effect on the body. Crying is a release and a good sign. It means a person is releasing anguish and is on the road to recovery.

Although crying is one of the best responses a grieving person can have, it is also one of the most embarrassing. Have you noticed how uncomfortable people become as soon as you begin to cry? They immediately shove a tissue at you as if to say, "Now stop it. Dry those eyes." Because of this reaction you hate for your tears to flow in front of others. If you begin to cry, you immediately apologize and try to stop.

At this stage in your life, you may feel compelled to put up a good front and not let anyone see your pain after your loved one has died. You may tend to deny needing help or comfort if anyone asks. It seems important that you not show anyone that you are hurting. You simply do not want to seem different.

Suzie told me, "I put up a good front for everyone but my best friend. She gave me the most comfort. We would sit in the spa at night and make up 'star stories.' We would look at the stars and say whatever came into our heads. Because it was dark, I didn't have to look at her, and it was like intense therapy. If my eyes teared, I just splashed water on my face and pretended it was drops of water running down. Without those nights I might never have been okay."

People who are grieving cry enough tears to fill bathtubs

to overflowing. The tears can come from sadness, anger, guilt, or even memories. They come often and unexpectedly. They flow as if they are beyond your control. Happiness brings tears, kindness brings tears, a hug brings tears. Everything or nothing at all causes tears to run down your cheeks at the oddest and most embarrassing moments. But the tears are nothing to be ashamed of—they are perfectly normal, natural, and healing.

Mood Swings

You are feeling hopeful and having a good time one minute, and then you are plunged into gloom the very next. You get so you do not know what to expect anymore. Mood swings are frequent for anyone who has suffered the death of someone close.

Sherry recalls, "I was in my formal all ready for the prom, feeling on top of the world, when my mother walked in the room with the camera. Dad had always taken the pictures before his death. I went from on top of the world to the depths of despair in the blink of an eye. My date couldn't understand why I was suddenly so quiet, but I think Mom realized by the look on my face. I pretended nothing was wrong, but at that moment I felt as if life would never be normal for me again."

That episode took place fifteen years ago. Sherry says she experienced a few bad moments similar to the prom episode on her wedding day. Her brother put out his arm to walk her down the aisle, and she felt winds of sadness blow by her. Fortunately, they passed quickly. Similarly, several years later she felt great sadness when she held her new baby boy in her arms and realized that he would never know his granddad.

"But life is good, too," she says. "I know how it feels to have only one parent, so I reach out to the kids at church when I hear about a divorce or a death in a family. I try to be their friend because I know the way they are hurting. I believe my dad's death made me more sensitive and compassionate. I really feel good when I can help these kids, and then I don't feel Dad's death was a complete waste."

Holidays

As if the challenge of everyday living is not enough, there have to be holidays.

"Holidays are the worst days of all. I wish I could cross them off the calendar," Randy declared.

Coping with the loss of a loved one takes an abundance of energy. It seems unfair that holidays have to slink about and add extra pressure and stress when each day is already an endurance test. But, fair or not, holidays will continue to arrive right on schedule. The ads, the store windows, your friends, will all remind you that the holiday season is approaching.

The most important way to approach a holiday or any special day is with a plan. You need to make plans in advance so you can stand firm and deal with the special day, instead of letting it come at you from behind, knocking you down. The plan itself is not important. *Having a plan is.* The plan can be to invite a friend to go to the beach with you to simply lie on the sand, soaking up the sun, relaxing and talking. It can be a plan to have lunch or dinner with someone special. It might be to take flowers to the cemetery or present a gift in memory of your loved one.

It is vitally important to spend the holidays with special, sensitive people who will understand that this is a difficult time for you. They need to be aware that you may not be the best of company at this time, but that you need them by your side.

Thanksgiving and Christmas can put a real strain on a

family who is missing a loved one. These are family times enveloped in memories.

It is a good idea to have a family discussion so everyone can express what they would like to see done for the holidays. Many families plan an entirely different type of day. A Christmas cruise or Thanksgiving in the woods cooking over a campfire can be good diversions. These new traditions may turn out to be some of the best ones in years to come. Keep your expectations low to avoid disappointment.

Tread very carefully around holidays. Doing the unexpected can cause alarm. One young man whose dad had died during the summer took a favorite photo and had it blown up and framed for his mother. Instead of being pleased with the present, she was devastated. Don't decide to show the old family videos without first asking if this will cause discomfort. When emotions are so close to the surface, it is best to be very careful.

Mother's and Father's Days can be equally difficult. The first year after my father died, I had to look away from the counters that displayed Father's Day cards. The second year I spotted a card with a great big slice of cheese on it. Dad and I had always had a joke between us about cheese. I bravely picked up the card and read it. It would have been perfect! The print kept blurring as a result of my tears, but instead of crying I said a prayer of thanks for the special person he had been. Death always comes too soon, whether we have had our loved one for fourteen or forty years.

When approaching Mother's or Father's Days, check with other family members and see what is expected of you. If they have no ideas, suggest something different from past years, possibly a visit with Grandma or a special aunt or uncle. If your family is not up to doing anything, make your own plans. Put a scrapbook in order, or read a good book. Clean your closet, or do something you never have time for otherwise. Your friends will probably all be busy with their own families, so you need to amuse yourself on this day.

"Why doesn't my mom remember that she's still a mother to me? All she did was cry all day long because my brother died last year." After a death there is no rhyme or reason for anyone's reactions. People are so fragile that the least thing can shatter them. Remind yourself that you are not responsible for your mother's tears. In time they will ease up. From now on life will be different. This is not to say it will always be sad. Sadness does not last forever. Little by little changes will take place in the family structure, and holidays will take on new meanings as the years go by.

Should birthdays still be celebrated? How about the birthday of the person who has died? Anniversaries? Should I get my mother an anniversary card after my dad dies? These are personal decisions. Give them advance thought.

Even though my father is no longer living, I still send my mother flowers and a card on her wedding anniversary to let her know I remember this special day. The first year it made her cry, but tears or not, she needed to know I hadn't forgotten. The cards I choose are not anniversary cards but rather cards that say, "I love you" or "Thinking of you today."

Valentine's Day can sometimes be a difficult holiday. As Randy approached Valentine's Day, he remembered the school secretary who had been especially sympathetic when his girlfriend had been killed in a car accident. Randy decided the secretary deserved a box of candy for Valentine's Day. He chose the biggest, frilliest, red satin heart-shaped box of candy he could find—the exact type his girlfriend had loved to receive.

"It was sad shopping for the candy, but in a way it was good, too. It gave me a chance to think about this year being different and that from now on every Valentine's Day would be different. When I handed the secretary the box and saw the way her face lit up, it made the sadness disappear for a while. I think I'll make this a memorial to Lori and buy candy for someone special every year."

Graduations, weddings, and other family times will all be different. Think them through in advance so that you can be prepared. Accept what cannot be changed and make the best of it. Try to keep communication lines open and let your loved ones know when you are uncomfortable with plans. Remember, nobody can read your mind.

An active church member said she received comfort during the holiday season from visiting a church other than the regular one she attended. The unfamiliar ceremony made her more alert and aware of the spirit working to heal her broken heart. She felt closer to the Lord while she was in church. *"The Lord is close to those whose hearts are breaking,"* (Ps. 34:18). She enjoyed the anonymity and did not feel forced to be sociable. Instead she communed exclusively with God.

Churches, like hospitals, are healing places. Surrounding yourself with familiar hymns, flickering candles, and stainedglass windows can be soothing to a troubled soul. God understands your pain when nobody else does. Don't be afraid to take it to him and allow him to share in carrying your heavy burden of pain.

Suicide

Approximately seven thousand teenagers kill themselves annually, almost twice as many as in the last decade. Many of these young adults came from good homes where they were surrounded by loving families. Unfortunately, for various reasons they felt hopeless and life became unbearable. In one awful instant, they chose to end their lives.

Deaths resulting from suicide leave behind them an astronomical amount of anger, guilt, and broken hearts. The loved ones who are left behind become victims, wondering, *How could a person I loved inflict such pain on me intentionally? Wasn't my love enough? How could I have stopped the death? Didn't I care enough to stop them?*

We must remind ourselves that the suicide victim had a choice and made it. Nobody else was responsible for that choice. Life became intolerable, and he or she chose to withdraw from it rather than face it. It was an individual decision that left many others feeling responsible and in agony.

If someone in your family commits suicide, you may wonder if you are suicidal too. Suicide is not hereditary. If your father committed suicide at age thirty-nine, that does not mean you will do the same thing. People who commit suicide are lost people who can see no hope left for themselves. Nobody could have changed what took place. All that the survivors can do is remove the blame from themselves and not destroy any additional lives. Talking about your feelings with a good friend, support group, or counselor may be necessary to resolve the anger and guilt. Don't be afraid to ask for help.

A suicide leaves many loose ends. It may be helpful to write a letter of farewell, saying all the things that were left unsaid by the sudden death. Most difficult of all, but most important, you must forgive the person for committing a most tragic act.

Robert Veninga, in his book *A Gift of Hope* (p. 263) states, "You may never condone that final self-destructive act. But a liberating feeling comes over you when you begin to understand that for your loved one death was the only recourse. . . . Your recovery will only begin when you give an unconditional pardon. And it will only end when you sense that your loved one is better off in death than in life."

3

Acceptance

Steve, whose best friend died when he was fourteen, said, "In the beginning stages of your grief, you'll feel overwhelmed by sadness. You wonder if this is the way you'll feel for the rest of your life. Intense sadness doesn't last forever. Soon a spark of hope will appear.

"Have you ever watched someone try to light a campfire when the wind was blowing? The wind blows the flame of the match out many times before a tiny spark will catch. That tiny spark will ignite and produce a bright, burning fire. Once the fire is burning, the wind can blow fiercely but it will no longer be able to put out the flames. All you need is a tiny spark of hope to get you started. The little spark will ignite and produce a bright, burning fire within. Once the hope returns, the winds of despair can no longer snuff it out."

When grief is worked through (instead of ignored), it will gently disappear until one day you will go for many hours

43

without feeling sad or thinking about your loved one who has died. This might bring feelings of guilt with it. Giving up the sadness, however, is not the same as giving up the person you loved. You are merely trading in the grief for loving memories. As long as the memories remain, the person is not gone from your life.

When happy memories replace the grief, an inner strength develops that will serve to make you stronger and your life more meaningful. But until your fire is burning brightly, it will be necessary to use whatever help is available. Just as it would be foolish to try to find your way along an unfamiliar path in complete darkness, it would be foolish to walk unaided with a broken spirit.

A torch that can light the way for broken hearts can come in the form of prayer. God promises to never leave us. He is our strength and our guiding light when we are stumbling about in the dark trying to find our way. "Your words are a flashlight to light the path ahead of me, and keep me from stumbling" (Ps. 119:105).

God's flashlight battery never runs out. Best of all, he knows what is in your heart, even when you cannot find the words to express it. He is always available, and his telephone line is never busy. Getting into the habit of talking with God in your own words is the best form of prayer. Asking for his help and turning to him for strength is so simple, yet so soothing.

In addition to the darkness, there are the roller coaster emotions. It is all right to ask God to take the controls and put you back on level ground. Healing is brought about from facing the loss, talking about it, and working on it. Contributing factors to healing are good nutrition, physical exercise, proper rest, expression of emotions, and advance preparation for holidays and special days.

Grieving is hard work and does not disappear with the

mere passage of time. Even with God's help, though, bitterness and unforgiveness can stand in the way of successful healing.

Releasing Bitterness

If you were given the choice between a chocolate candy bar and a square of unsweetened cooking chocolate, which would you choose? Me, too. I'd grab that candy bar so fast you wouldn't see it disappear! The difference between the two chocolates is in the sweetening. Life, too, can be sweet or bitter. The choice is up to you.

In the early days of mourning it is natural to question, "Why me?" and to wish you had not been singled out for this loss. It is perfectly normal to feel sorry for yourself. As time passes it is necessary to steer yourself in a direction that will ease you out of that rut. Granted, you cannot change the circumstances, but you can use them to make life better. Remember, the difference between being bitter and being better is all in the *I*.

What can *I* do with my life to make it better? First you can change the "Why me?" question to a "How" question. "How can I become stronger as a result of this tragedy?" or "How can I put this experience to good use?" All "Why" questions can be turned into constructive statements when changed into "How's." Next, you can rid yourself of bad feelings toward others. If you grab on to a grudge against the doctor, the drunk driver, or your remaining parent, you will only bring about more sadness in your own life. Bitterness and unforgiveness hurt only the people who hold them. It belongs to them. The party they feel is deserving of their bitterness often does not even know it exists. So it attaches itself like a parasite, eating away at the one who holds it, taking away that person's joy, peace, and good feelings. At the same time the person who supposedly caused it walks around blissfully, content, unaware of the parasite's existence.

It does not make any sense to continue to allow this parasite to hold you in its clutches. It has to be torn away before the peace that is rightfully yours can surface.

How is this done? There are various methods that can work for getting rid of unforgiveness or bitterness.

1. Fold a piece of paper in half. On one side list the positive results occurring from your bitterness. On the other side list the negative ones. Be fair and honest. When the list is complete, look it over, and decide if it is worth hanging on to your grudge. If not, tear it up and toss away both the grudge and the shredded paper.

2. Find a trusted friend to talk with about your bitterness. Often merely verbalizing these negative feelings will clear them up in your own mind, and you will then be free to take the necessary steps to discard them.

3. When you are all alone, place an empty chair across from you. Pretend the person you are angry with is sitting in the chair. Tell that person your feelings. Express your anger. This may sound silly, but it *does* work.

Forgiving Others (and Ourselves)

"I never thought much about the drunk driver who killed Scott," Jamie said. "My problem was with forgiving myself for not being with him the day he was killed. I would go over and over in my mind all the things that would have changed if I had gone to school that day. For instance, I walk slower than Scott, so we would not have been on that particular corner at the exact moment the car came by. I could make myself sick to my stomach just thinking about it. Eventually I told another friend my feelings and she pointed out how silly I was being. From then on, every time those thoughts began to plague me, what I did was remind myself, very emphatically, that I could not change the past."

Forgiving ourselves is just as important as forgiving others. Holding ourselves responsible when it is too late to change a situation is fruitless and disabling. To heal, you need to forgive yourself for your mistakes. Unforgiveness can eat away at your insides, hurting only you. It will keep the hurt from healing, making it fester. "Forgive and forget" is not just a catchy phrase. Those two words are linked together because one without the other is meaningless. To truly forgive means also to forget.

How is it possible to forget? We need more than our own resources to draw on when trying to forget a great injustice. We need to pray for guidance as we set our goals toward forgiving. And we can pray for our enemies, as the Bible suggests. When we do so, incredible events begin to take place. While trying to forgive and forget, it is often profitable to look at those around us who have let unforgiveness destroy their joy. You will notice that these people cannot advance toward fulfilled lives until the barriers of bitterness and unforgiveness are removed.

Internal Dialogue

The way we talk to ourselves affects our attitude. We all talk to ourselves. We say things to ourselves that we would not say to anyone else. We say, "You can't do anything right," "You're stupid," or "Life is not worth living." If we make these negative statements often enough, we begin to believe them.

When a person is in mourning, the negative thoughts erupt constantly. You need to become alert to these thoughts and listen attentively. Then you should consciously change the negative statements to positive ones. When you say good things to yourself you will begin to believe them, and they will become true: "Today is going to be better." "I look pretty good today." "I feel good!" Take control of your thoughts and do not let them control you any longer. "I yam, what I yam, what I yam," said Popeye. He said he was powerful and he believed it. Tell yourself you are wonderful and believe it. Look at yourself in the mirror and say, "Today is going to be a good day!"

Laughter

Nobody can be sad twenty-four hours a day. It would be unhealthy and unnatural. But when you do find yourself laughing or enjoying yourself, you feel guilty. Yet laughter is a healing balm that can be used to repair a hurting heart.

Teri said, "When my aunt died many relatives who I had not seen in a long time came to California. The funeral was like a big family reunion. I loved these family members and really enjoyed seeing them again. I caught myself laughing with glee when a cousin I had not seen in several years walked into the funeral home. I was really embarrassed and ashamed of my reaction afterward. "Looking back, I know my aunt wouldn't have minded. She would have been happy about the way we all loved each other and enjoyed being together." Teri wasn't being disrespectful, she was just reinforcing her sadness with strong beams of love.

In addition to surrounding yourself with special people you love, sometimes a silly movie, a humorous book, or a tape done by your favorite comedian can bring about some relief from the constant mourning. It is healthy to laugh as long as it is not done in the presence of another person who is also suffering and may not be ready for a lightening of the mood at exactly the same moment you are. Laughter relieves stress and releases natural painkillers in the body that help you feel better emotionally. Studies have shown that physically ill people heal faster when they are subjected to daily bouts of laughter.

Music

Music is also a natural stress reliever. It can lift us up, bring us down, cause haunting memories, or heal our hurting hearts. Music speaks to us in ways that words cannot. Choose your music wisely while you are recovering. It can play a big part in the healing process.

Megan, whose friend died of cancer, said, "When my special friend, Jodi, was dying, I bought two tapes for her. But she died that day before I got to the hospital, so I never had a chance to give them to her. I planned to return them to the store but never seemed to get around to it. One day I took them out of the package and played one. It made my spirit soar. From then on I thought of those as Jodi's tapes. Whenever I am especially missing her, I listen to one and it makes me feel better."

Creating your own music, if you have talent in that direction, is another way to soothe yourself. Many of the most touching, lasting songs have evolved through a mist of pain as the artist released feelings from a depth that is only achieved from despair.

Likewise, playing a person's favorite music after they have died can make you feel close to them again.

Creative Tasks

Any creative activity can relieve suffering, whether it is composing a song, writing a poem, painting a picture, creating a story, or sewing a quilt. It does not have to be a world masterpiece to be shared. It is the act of doing and creating that brings the comfort, not the finished product. Because I am a writer I feel compelled to write about important events in my life. Any episode of importance is incomplete until I have captured it on paper. It is as if the camera has frozen in time a frame of my life and no forward movement is possible until the words are written down. Then I can lay it aside with a sigh and say, "*Finis*, done, finished, the end."

Communication

Nothing is more important than communication. "Great, but how can you communicate if nobody wants to listen?" This is a common problem. Many people feel so uncomfortable with the subject of death that they back away from it. They actually want to help, but they simply do not know how. To fill these gaps, support groups are forming in many communities. In a support group you are surrounded with others who have similar experiences and problems. The other members know exactly what you are going through and provide an opportunity where you can feel comfortable talking about death. Check your local newspaper for support groups or call the local hospitals or churches. If there are not any, call your local chapter of the American Cancer Society or other organizations and ask if one can be started in your area.

Sarah, following the death of her brother, discovered a technique for opening the lines of communication with others. "You have to be willing to make the first move. Nobody will realize you need help unless you are willing to share your pain. You have to venture out from behind your mask that says everything is just fine, and find people who are not uncomfortable with your sharing."

School counselors may also be able to start support groups that meet during lunch hour. Talking to the school counselor on a one-to-one basis can also be a great help. Pastors, youth group leaders, or teachers are often willing to help. They have resources to draw upon that you might not even be aware of, such as a person with a loss similar to yours. Don't be afraid to ask them for help.

Following the drowning of his twin brother, Jeff said, "I know I need to talk to someone. When I mention my brother around my mom, she cries. When I try to talk to my friends, they get funny looks on their faces and get real quiet. What am I supposed to do?" Try Sarah's method, and keep searching.

Often when a parent dies, the remaining parent is too devastated to be of much support, making it necessary to look beyond your own home. Jason's dad died suddenly of a heart attack. "I feel like I'm all alone. Mom is so busy grieving, I don't think she remembers she has a son. I don't want to bother her with my problems on top of everything else." Aunts and uncles, cousins, or teachers can sometimes fill the void until the remaining parent is stronger. The difficult part is searching for help and being willing to allow that person to help you.

Feeling alone and being alone with your grief are not good. Scripture tells us that, "Two can accomplish more than twice as much as one, for the results will be much better. If one falls, the other pulls him up; but if a man falls when he is alone, he is in trouble" (Eccles 4:9).

Physical contact feels good when we are hurting—hugs, pats on the back, a neck massage, someone holding your hand. Jason admitted, "I sure could have used some hugs, but no way would I ask for them!"

Don't be afraid to ask for a hug. An interesting fact is that when you reach out your arms to hug someone, you receive a hug in return. Hugs feel good!

Creative Imagery

Andy was the class clown. His grades were poor, he did not get along with the other students, and he was a real problem to his teacher, Mr. Jones.

There was a special exercise that Mr. Jones liked to use with his students. He called it *creative imagery*. He had the class sit quietly and close their eyes. He told them to picture themselves in a specific situation that they wished to be in. They could picture someone with them if they needed another person to guide them through the task. They were to fully participate in the activity, step by step, and he gave them plenty of time to accomplish it.

Afterward he asked if anyone wished to share their experience with the class. Over the years he had heard about students flying airplanes, going to the moon, winning Olympic medals in the diving competition, hiking to the tops of mountains, and walking across the stage after being crowned Miss America. Creative imagery proved to be a favorite with the students and the teacher.

One year it proved to be even more than that.

It had been a difficult school year, the one with the class clown. Mr. Jones was hesitant about even attempting the creative imagery, wondering if the class would settle down and be serious enough to participate. One day he tried it.

Much to his surprise, when he asked who wanted to share, Andy eagerly raised his hand. Hesitantly, Mr. Jones called on him. Andy stood up and said, "You all know my mother was sick a long time, and she died last year. Well, they wouldn't let me see her or go to the funeral. I had to stay at a friend's house. Today I went to her funeral. She looked nice and peaceful. She wasn't hurting anymore. Everyone was crying when they looked at her, and I cried too. It made me feel sad but it made me feel good too. I wanted to be there." A hush fell over the classroom as he spoke. Nobody snickered; nobody nudged each other. Some of the kids studied their hands or their shoes as Andy spoke, but they all listened.

Andy went on to say, "You wouldn't believe how much better I feel now. I feel like a big, heavy weight has been lifted off me."

Mr. Jones was taken by complete surprise. He had known about the death but never expected Andy to expose his pain before the entire class. The result was almost instantaneous, more like fiction than real life. Andy began to get along better with his classmates, his grades improved, and he no longer seemed to need the negative attention he had been seeking.

Not all situations have as happy an ending as Andy's, but creative imagery can be used by anyone at anytime. It can be used to bring comfort from events that cannot be changed. It can be used to say good-bye to a loved one who died suddenly. It can be used to walk yourself through a difficult situation before it occurs. Tuck it in your toolbox to be used when necessary.

Relaxation

It is absolutely essential to your well-being to learn how to relax. When you leave a car in first gear for too long, you can hear it grinding as it waits to be shifted. The same with second gear. It strains until you shift it into third gear. Finally, in fourth gear, you can hear that the engine has leveled off, and the motor is purring along nicely.

Listen to your body and shift into the gear that takes the least strain. Just like your car, it will need less repairs and will last longer if it is driven gently. Treat yourself tenderly. Take time out for relaxation, laughter, and creative activities that bring personal rewards, and reach out to others in communication.

Breathing deeply is one of the best ways to calm yourself and bring about relaxation. Long sighs may sound like distress signals, but they are one of the body's natural relaxation techniques. Allow yourself to sigh when you begin to feel stressed.

Sarah shared her special breathing exercise: "Simply breathe slowly through your nose, expanding your abdomen and then your rib cage. Next, release the breath through your nose more slowly than you took it in, silently counting up to eight. Do this several times until you feel your body beginning to relax. Try it, it's great!"

A brisk walk is another simple way to help the body relax. Walk with a friend for double therapy and have a heart-to-heart talk while you are walking. Add some laughter for triple therapy.

"My dog and I have wonderful walks," said Kevin. "I tell him all my problems as we walk in deserted areas and he never interrupts. I make sure nobody else is around, though, because they might not understand."

Another item high in therapeutic value is water. Water has a soothing effect on the mind and body. The weightless feeling in the water can make relaxing easier. During the summer months, put an inner tube around your waist and float aimlessly in a swimming pool, or head for the beach and listen to the waves as they lap over your feet. When cool weather sets in and outdoor water therapy is no longer possible, fill the bathtub with comfortably hot water, add some fragrant bubble bath, and then submerge yourself up to your chin. Let your arms drift weightlessly to the surface, inhale the aroma, and enjoy!

Or maybe you are a shower person. Let the warm water beat on the back of your neck to release the tension. Force yourself to sing a cheerful song while the water drowns out the sound. Towel yourself off briskly to get the circulation going. Only when your body is in a relaxed state can it work on recovering. Emotions that are bruised need to be given a chance to heal instead of being pounded on continually. Be kind and gentle with yourself while you are healing, and don't be afraid to pamper yourself.

Acceptance

As your battered emotions begin to heal, the season of grief will subside. How long will this process take? When will this hurting end? These are questions that have no answers. Each individual has a personal time clock unlike anyone else's. It is important to know that your grief is yours alone and cannot be compared with your brother's or anyone else's grief process. The intensity of the pain will lessen gradually, often without an awareness that it is happening, until one day a spark of hope will ignite and you will notice that joy is again part of your life. When this happens, each of the stages and tasks mentioned in this book will become easier to do. The season of hope will not be far away. The isolated good moments will turn into entire days, making you want to strive to feel good more often. And you will. Sadness *does* disappear. Facing grief, mourning the loss, acknowledging your feelings, expressing anger, working to bring about forgiveness, and adjusting to the changes in life will result in acceptance. The grief will diminish, but the love and memories will remain.

With the arrival of acceptance you will be able to reach out and use your experience to help others and further aid in your own regeneration. Steve Brown, a pastor in Key Biscayne, Florida, tells of the day news of a family death reached him when he was speaking at a church in Tennessee. The church's stout preacher walked over and enfolded Steve in a huge hug. "Use this pain," he said "because for every ten people you meet, seven of them will have a broken heart."

When your broken heart mends, you will no longer be the same. You will never be the same again. You will be *stronger*. This experience can be put to use, and this new strength can be used for the rest of your life to reach out and help others whose broken hearts are fresh and new.

Epilogue

One year later Anne says she takes life one day at a time, with some days being better than others. It's been a year heavy with changes and many adjustments. She moved in with her Aunt Barbara and attended a different high school. She made new friends, and fortunately the school adjustment was no problem. "I'm doing okay," she says.

Suggested Reading List

Buscaglia, Leo. *The Fall of Freddie the Leaf.* Thorofare, NJ: Charles B. Slack Inc., 1982.
>   Written for a young child but clearly defines the stages of life.

Deits, Bob. *Life After Loss.* Tucson, AZ: Fisher Books, 1988.
>   Lists things that can be done to ease the pain of loss.

Kolf, June Cerza. *How Can I Help?* Grand Rapids, MI: Baker Book House, 1989.
>   Suggests ways to help others get through grief.

_____. *When Will I Stop Hurting?* Grand Rapids, MI: Baker Book House, 1987.
>   Identifies stages of grief and ways to understand it.

Mcginnis, Alan Loy. *The Friendship Factor.* Minneapolis, MN: Augsburg Publishing House, 1979.
>   Insights on having and being a good friend.

Peck, M. Scott, M.D. *The Road Less Traveled.* New York: Simon & Schuster, 1978.
>   Shows how to face reality and achieve serenity in life.

Smedes, Lewis B. *Forgive and Forget.* San Francisco: Harper & Row, 1984.
>   Walks through the four stages of forgiveness: hurting, hating, healing, and reconciliation.

Veninga, Robert L. *A Gift of Hope.* New York: Ballantine Books, 1985.
>   Excellent section on suicide. Deals with losses of all kinds.

Wright, H. Norman. *Beating the Blues.* Ventura, CA: Regal Books, 1988.
>   Helps to recognize depression and offers steps to conquer it.